S0-FFP-860

an easy-read ACTIVITY book

MUSICAL INSTRUMENTS YOU CAN MAKE

by PHYLLIS HAYES

illustrated by Dennis Kendrick

Franklin Watts
New York/London/Toronto/Sydney
1981

To my family

R.L. 3.2 Spache Revised Formula

Library of Congress Cataloging in Publication Data
Hayes, Phyllis.
Musical instruments you can make.

(An easy-read activity book)
Summary: Instructions for making a variety of musical instruments from such items as paper plates, bottles, electric light bulbs, coffee cans, and rubber bands.

1. Musical instruments—Construction—Juvenile literature. [1. Musical instruments—Construction] I. Kendrick, Dennis. II. Title. III. Series: Easy-read activity book.
ML3930.A2H325   781.91   81-856
ISBN 0-531-04310-X   AACR2

Text copyright © 1981 by Phyllis Hayes
Illustrations copyright © 1981 by Dennis Kendrick
All rights reserved
Printed in the United States of America
6 5 4 3 2 1

Contents

Turn a Comb into a Harmonica	6
Make a Water Glass Chime	8
An Empty Coffee Can Makes a Good Drum	11
Make Maracas from Electric Light Bulbs	14
Paper Plates Make Good Shakers	18
Make Flutes from Bottles	21
Make a Simple Kazoo	24
Rock with a Cigar Box Guitar	26
Make Music Outdoors with Garden Gongs	29
We Hear Many Sounds in an Orchestra	32

It is fun to listen or dance to music. And you can enjoy music in a special way when you make music with instruments that you have made yourself.

Music begins with sound. You can make music by causing air to move. This is called **vibration** (vye-BRAY-shun).

You can see how vibration and sound work together. Take a rubber band and loop it over two fingers. Spread your fingers to make the rubber band stretch.

Use the index or "pointer" finger on your other hand to strum across the stretched rubber band. The humming sound that you hear is made by the rubber band moving against the air.

SPIKE

Turn a Comb into a Harmonica

Another name for the **harmonica** (har-MON-uh-kuh) is the mouth organ. The harmonica is made up of strips of cane or metal inside a case. These strips are called **reeds**. There are blowholes on the outside of the case. When you blow air into the holes, the air causes the reeds to vibrate and sound is made.

You need:
scissors
a piece of wax paper
a fine-toothed comb

How to Do It:
1. Cut the wax paper so that it is the same length as the comb. Make sure the paper is wide enough to cover both sides of the teeth of the comb.
2. Hold the comb so the teeth are pointing up.
3. Fold the wax paper over the top of the teeth.

4. Hold the comb on both ends.

5. Put your mouth against the side of the comb and blow into the comb. Make a "ha-ha" sound.

6. Now you can blow a song you like into the comb harmonica. You should be able to feel the air vibrating against your lips.

Make a Water Glass Chime

Most chimes are made of metal bells or hollow tubes. Chimes can also be shaped like rectangles or beehives. Each bell in the chime has a different **pitch** (the highness or lowness of a sound). The amount of vibration in each bell will make its pitch high or low.

You need:
five drinking glasses, all the same size
   and at least 6 inches (15.24 cm) tall
water
a spoon

How to Do It:
1. Line the glasses up. In the first glass, pour ½ to 1 inch (1.32 to 2.64 cm) of water.
2. Pour 2 inches (5.08 cm) of water in the second glass.
3. Pour 3 inches (7.62 cm) in the third glass.

4. Pour 4 inches (10.16 cm) in the fourth glass.

5. Pour 5 inches (12.70 cm) in the fifth glass.

6. Lightly tap each glass with the spoon.

7. Play a simple tune you know by tapping the sides of the glasses with the spoon. If the tune doesn't sound right, you can change the pitch by adding or taking out water.

What happens when you add more water? The pitch will be lower. Why? Because the more water you add, the less vibration there will be in the glass.

An Empty Coffee Can Makes a Good Drum

Long ago, drums were simple hollow logs beaten with sticks. Later, they were made from tree trunks. Animal skins were used to cover hollow tree trunks to make the drum "head." Drums have also been made from clay, wood, or metal barrels and from sea turtle shells.

You need:
a coffee can with a plastic lid
heavy paper
scissors
crayons or markers
tape or glue
a small stick or wooden spoon

How to Do It:
1. Cut the paper so that it fits on the outside of the can.
2. Use crayons or markers to decorate the paper.
3. Wrap the paper around the can and tape or glue the edges together. If you use glue, let the drum dry for one day.

4. Use the stick or spoon for a drumstick.
5. Because the drum has both a metal and a plastic "head," you can make many different kinds of sounds.

Make Maracas from Electric Light Bulbs

South Americans often use the **maraca** (muh-ROCK-uh) to make their music more lively. Long ago, the maraca was made from a dried, hard-shelled fruit called a gourd. The gourd was filled with seeds or small stones.

Here is an easy way to make your own maraca—from a burned-out electric light bulb. You can shake the maraca in the air or hit it against your hand or leg.

You need:
newspaper
¼ cup (60 ml) white glue
¼ cup (60 ml) water
a mixing bowl
a burned-out electric light bulb
a small piece of wax paper
acrylic paint

How to Do It:

1. Spread some of the newspaper on a table.
2. Mix the glue and water together in a mixing bowl.

3. Tear the rest of the paper into short strips and soak them in the glue mixture for a few minutes.

4. Lay the strips of newspaper on the light bulb until the bulb is completely covered. Be sure to cover the metal base as well.

5. Put on several layers of paper. Carefully smooth the wrinkles with your fingers.
6. Set the bulb on the piece of wax paper so it won't stick. Let the bulb dry in a sunny place for one day. The bulb is dry when the paper covering is completely hard.
7. Ask a grown-up to drop the dry, paper-covered bulb gently on firm ground or concrete. The outer, hard paper covering will not break, but the inside will. The broken glass inside your maraca will be the "rattles."
8. Paint the maraca with acrylic paint if you like. Paint makes the maraca brighter and also stronger.

Paper Plates Make Good Shakers

Shakers are easily made from many different things. The **tambourine** (TAM-ber-een) is both a shaker and a shallow drum. It has a round frame with metal circles that are fastened to it. When you hit a tambourine with your hand, it will make a jingling sound. Not all shakers are round. American Indians used to make shakers by fastening small bones and shells together.

You need:
two strong paper plates
a hole punch
crayons or markers
uncooked beans, peas, macaroni, or rice
cord

How to Do It:
1. Set one plate on a table. Turn the other plate upside down and put it on top of the first plate.

2. Put your hand on the top plate to hold both plates together.

3. Use the hole punch to put holes ½ inch (1.32 cm) apart all around the plate edges.

4. Separate the plates. Decorate the outsides of both plates with crayons or markers.

5. Put a few spoonfuls of beans, peas, macaroni, or rice inside one plate.

6. Turn the other plate upside down again and set it on top. Match the holes on the two plates.

7. Use the cord to lace the two plates together. Be sure you leave about 6 inches (15.24 cm) of cord at both ends so you can tie the ends together when you have laced all the holes.

8. You can shake or hit the shaker with your hand.

9. You and your friends can make several shakers with a different kind of "rattle" in the plates. A rice shaker has a much softer sound than one filled with macaroni or beans.

Make Flutes from Bottles

We know many things about the days when people lived in caves because of the drawings they made on the walls. Some drawings show that they made musical horns from the horns of animals and flutes from bone and wood.

You need:
several different size empty bottles (water or soda bottles, liquid shortening or oil bottles, large juice bottles, catsup bottles, or jugs)

How to Do It:
1. Put the top edge of an empty bottle against your lower lip.

2. Blow across the top of the bottle. Some of the air will go into the bottle and move around inside your "flute."

3. Arrange your bottles according to sizes. You can make an instrument that works like the water glass chime.

4. You will discover that the big bottles have a low pitch. The smaller bottles have a high pitch.

Make a Simple Kazoo

The **kazoo**, or voice mask, works something like the comb harmonica. *You* have to make the sounds. The kazoo will disguise your voice to make it sound more like a real musical instrument.

You need:
wax paper
scissors
an empty cardboard tube
a rubber band

How to Do It:

1. Cut a 6-inch (15.24-cm) circle of wax paper.
2. Put the wax paper over one end of the tube.
3. Wrap the rubber band around the wax paper to hold it in place.
4. Hum a tune into the open end of the tube.

Rock with a Cigar Box Guitar

Guitars are string instruments that were first used in Egypt a long time ago. Today, people play the guitar all over the world. You have probably heard the guitar played as part of folk music, jazz, or modern rock bands.

You need:

a knife
a cardboard cigar box
a ruler
a pencil
four rubber bands, each one a different
  thickness

How to Do It:

1. Ask a grown-up to take off the box lid with a knife.

2. On one short side of the box, use the ruler to measure 1 inch (2.64 cm) from one end of the box. Mark this place with your pencil.

3. Measure 1 inch (2.64 cm) from the first mark and again mark it with your pencil.

4. Make two more pencil marks, each 1 inch (2.64 cm) apart from the one before it.

5. Measure and mark the other short side of the box the same way. You should have four pencil marks on each short end.

6. Ask a grown-up to help you cut a small notch in each of the places where you have a pencil mark.

7. Starting on one end, stretch the thickest rubber band across the open top of the box. Fit the rubber band in the end notch on both sides of the box. The rubber band must fit tightly around the box.

8. Take the next thickest rubber band and do the same thing in the next notch on both ends.

9. Repeat this with the other two rubber bands. Be sure you have the thinnest rubber band on the end.

10. Strum the bands lightly with your fingers. Which rubber band has the lowest pitch? Which has the highest?

Make Music Outdoors with Garden Gongs

The gong is a round, flat instrument which hangs on a stand. It is often made out of a metal called bronze. The gong makes a deep tone when hit with a hammer. Many years ago the gong was used in the Orient to call people to prayer services and to signal other important events.

Today, gongs are used as musical instruments in orchestras. Electric gongs are used for fire and burglar alarms.

Gongs don't have to be made from metal. You can use clay flowerpots.

You need:
three clay flowerpots (small, medium, and large)
paints or markers
cord
scissors
a wooden spoon

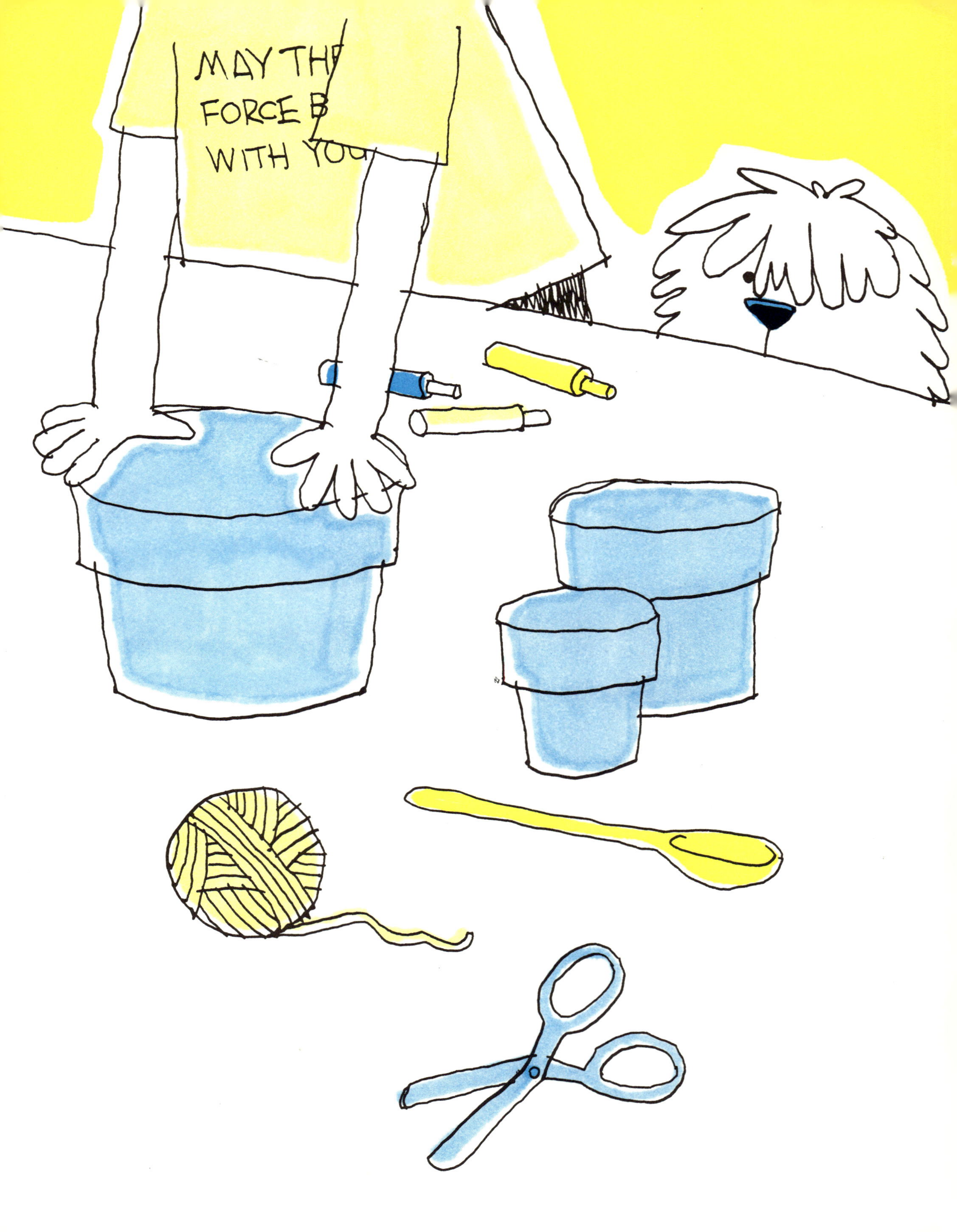
MAY THE
FORCE B
WITH YOU

How to Do It:

1. Decorate the pots with paint or markers.

2. Make a knot in each piece of cord. The knot should be large enough so that it will not slip out of the flowerpot hole.

3. Pull the cord up through the inside of each pot, so the knot will be inside.

4. Arrange the pots in order, from the one that will have the highest pitch to the one with the lowest. The small pot will have the highest pitch.

5. Tie the pots to a tree branch. Be sure they all hang from the same height, at least 12 inches (30.48 cm).

6. Hit each pot lightly with the spoon.

We Hear Many Sounds in an Orchestra

An **orchestra** (OR-kes-truh) is a group of musicians who play many different instruments. You may want to start an orchestra with your friends. Making your own instruments is easy and fun. Each of you can play the instrument you enjoy most.